Contents

Words in **bold** are in the glossary on page 31.

Creative thinking

Craft has never been so cool! Everyone's designing, making and **customising**. This book shows you how to turn old clothes into something new, and stamp your own style on them.

Get the gear!

Besides using your own old clothes, look in charity shops and jumble sales for fabulous finds. You may have basic sewing items, such as pins, needles, thread and scissors, at home. If not, you can buy them at craft shops or department stores – along with a range of fabrics and **haberdashery**, such as beads, buttons, ribbons and trimmings.

Why do it?

When you customise your clothes, you can express yourself and have things just the way you want them. You save money too, and learn skills that could even lead to a crafty career.

Safety

Remember to keep strings, cords and sharp things like pins, needles and scissors away from small children.

Tip!

If you have a sewing machine and know how it works, you can use it for some of the projects in this book.

Tip!
Look for a shoebox, food container or toolbox to store all your sewing stuff and your **'stash'** in. That's the crafty name for your collection of favourite fabrics, beads and trimmings.

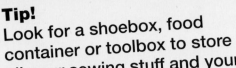

You're the boss

Remember, you don't need to follow all the instructions in this book exactly. If you like, just use the methods and ideas to come up with your own creations.

It's green as well!

Customising is a great way to recycle. You can jazz up things you're bored with, rework clothes that are worn out or don't fit, and use up fabric scraps and other odds and ends. Just remember to check with whoever buys your clothes before slicing up or decorating half of your wardrobe!

T-shirt picture

With this simple method, you can sew a picture onto a T-shirt, vest, hoodie or whatever you like. It works best on plain, flat fabrics.

- T-shirt or other **garment**
- Pencil and paper
- Needle with a large eye
- **Embroidery** thread (also called stranded cotton) in a bright colour
- Scissors
- **Sewing chalk**

1 First, sketch your design on paper. Start with something easy, such as a star, a heart, a piece of fruit or a bug.

2 Copy the design lightly onto the T-shirt using a pencil or sewing chalk.

3 Cut a piece of embroidery thread about 50cm long. Thread the needle (lick the end of the thread to make it easier) and tie a knot at the long end.

4 Push the needle through from the inside of the T-shirt at the start of your design. Then, holding one hand inside the T-shirt, sew neatly along the line, using **backstitch** (see box below).

Tip!
Use backstitch when you need to make a strong seam or **hem**.

5 When you've finished, sew through to the inside of the T-shirt again, tie a knot and snip the thread.

How to do backstitch

1 Push the needle tip in and out of the fabric, making a small stitch.

2 Go back to where the thread disappears into the fabric and push the needle in.

3 Do another stitch, coming out a bit further along.

4 Do the same with each stitch, going back to fill in the space left by the stitch before.

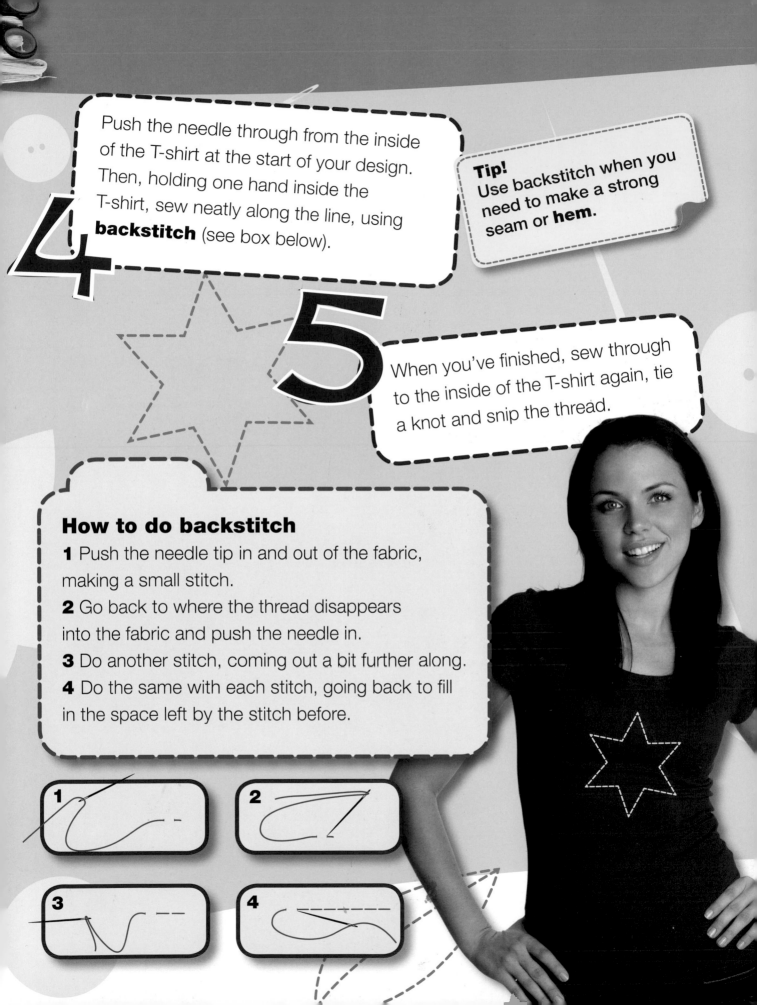

Ribbons and trimmings

Glam up a boring top, jeans, hoodie or anything you like by sewing on a ribbon, decorative trimming or lace edging.

Get the gear!

- Clothes you want to customise
- Needles, pins and sewing thread
- Scissors
- Ribbons and trimmings

1 To add a ribbon trim to a V-neck top, you'll need about 1m of ribbon. Starting at the back of your top, lay the ribbon along the edge of the fabric, and pin it in place. Work all the way around to where you started.

2 To go around a V-neck point, fold the ribbon over itself like this.

3 To finish, trim the ribbon to a little longer than you need, fold the end over and pin it on top of the other end.

How to do overstitch

1 Thread your needle and knot the end of the thread.

2 Poke the needle tip under the edge you want to sew, push it through both fabrics, and pull towards you.

3 Move the needle along slightly and do the same again. Keep stitching like this all the way around, then knot the thread and snip off.

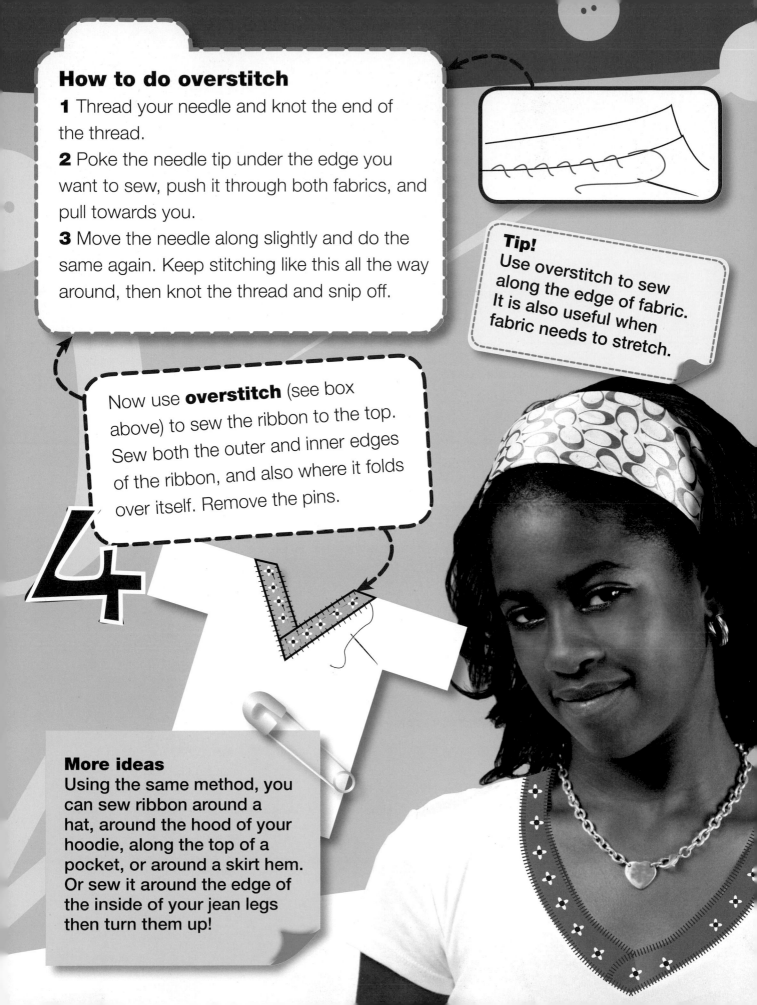

Tip!
Use overstitch to sew along the edge of fabric. It is also useful when fabric needs to stretch.

Now use **overstitch** (see box above) to sew the ribbon to the top. Sew both the outer and inner edges of the ribbon, and also where it folds over itself. Remove the pins.

4

More ideas
Using the same method, you can sew ribbon around a hat, around the hood of your hoodie, along the top of a pocket, or around a skirt hem. Or sew it around the edge of the inside of your jean legs then turn them up!

Felt flowers

Attach these funk-tastic flowers to a cardie, a dress or your favourite woolly hat.

Get the gear!

- 2 or 3 squares of thick felt
- Selection of buttons
- Pencil, scissors and a needle
- Extra-strong thread

1

To make one flower, draw a flower outline on one piece of felt. On a contrasting colour, draw a smaller circle that will fit inside the flower.

Tip!
You could draw around a coin or a button to help you make a perfect circle.

2

Cut out both pieces and lay the circle on top of the petals. Choose a button and pop it right in the middle.

3

Cut some thread, thread your needle and tie a knot in the end of the thread.

How to sew on a button

Thread a needle and knot the end of the thread. Sew in from the back or inside of your fabric or garment. Stick the needle through one hole in the button, back through the other hole and through the fabric again. Sew in and out through both holes about 10 times. Knot and snip off the thread at the back of the fabric.

4

Holding the three parts in position, sew them together through the holes on the button (see box above).

5

Now it's ready to attach! Sew it where you want it to go – or fix with a safety pin if you want it to be detachable.

Jazz up your jeans

Add some decoration to your denim jeans to turn them into something really special.

Get the gear!

- Needles, thread, scissors, pencil and paper
- Embroidery thread
- Buttons, **sequins** or beads (check first the holes are big enough for a needle)
- Sewing chalk

Pocket picture

1 Use the method on pages 6–7 to sew a picture or **slogan** (or both!) onto a jeans pocket. Bright or light colours will stand out best.

2 For extra impact, sew around the shape a few times in different colours. You can also add buttons, beads or sequins.

Tip!

Sewing onto a pocket or leg can be a bit awkward. Scrunch up the edge of the pocket or the end of the leg, so you can hold one hand at the back of the fabric while you sew.

12

Growing on you

1

A growing, spreading flower plant design like this one can grow up (or down) your leg! Practise on paper first; then use sewing chalk to draw the design on your jeans.

2

Use embroidery thread to backstitch (see page 7) along the curling stems, and a different colour (or beads) for flowers.

Tip!
To sew on a bead, push your needle through from the back of the fabric first; then thread it through the bead's hole. Sew back and forth through the hole and the fabric several times. Finally, knot tightly at the back.

Chic corsage

A **corsage** is a small bouquet of flowers worn on your clothes. These fabric flowers look great on a belt, hat or dress and are easy to make. Wear one to make a bold statement or put a few together for a bouquet.

Get the gear!

- Strip of fabric, about 10cm wide and 50cm long
- Needle, scissors and thread

Tip!
Experiment with different fabrics. Plain, silky material makes a good rose, or use printed cotton for a funky or folky flower.

1 First, fold the strip of fabric in half lengthways.

2 Thread the needle and knot one end of the thread. Sew the edges of the strip together, about 1cm in, using **running stitch** (see box below) with quite large stitches (about 1cm long).

How to do running stitch

Running stitch is a very simple stitch where you simply sew in and out of the fabric in a straight line. It is most useful for sewing thick fabrics, **gathering** fabrics or to make a decorative stitch.

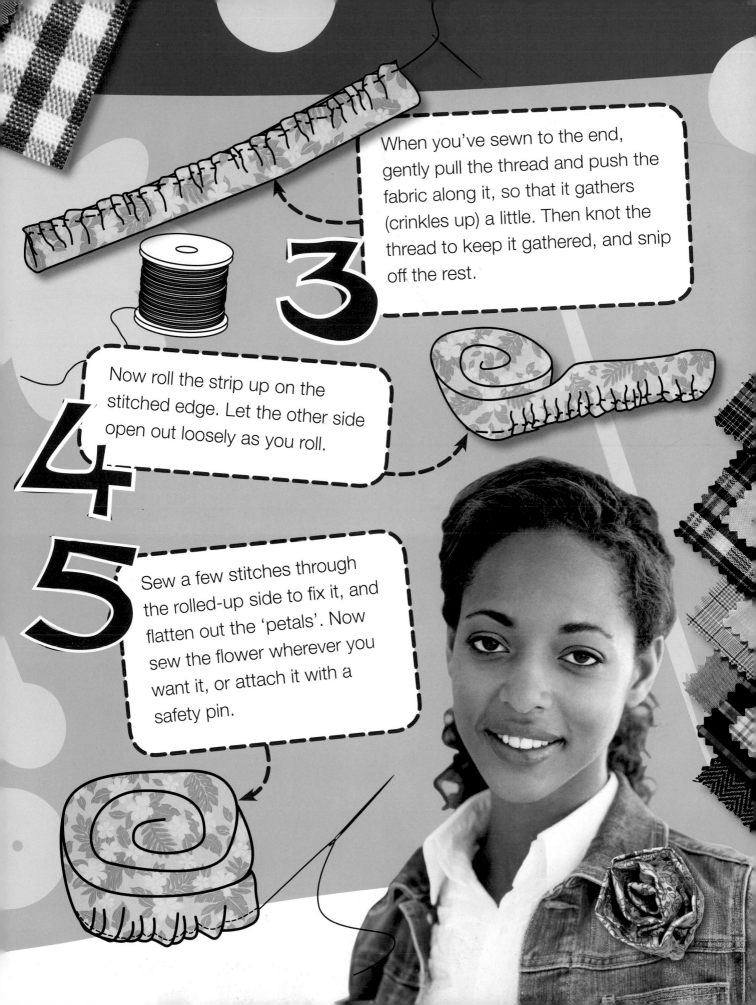

3 When you've sewn to the end, gently pull the thread and push the fabric along it, so that it gathers (crinkles up) a little. Then knot the thread to keep it gathered, and snip off the rest.

4 Now roll the strip up on the stitched edge. Let the other side open out loosely as you roll.

5 Sew a few stitches through the rolled-up side to fix it, and flatten out the 'petals'. Now sew the flower wherever you want it, or attach it with a safety pin.

Trousers to shorts

When the knees on your jeans get a big hole in them, turn them into shorts instead!

Get the gear!

- Old jeans
- Tape measure or ruler
- Scissors, pins, needles and extra-strong thread

1 Put the jeans on and decide how long you want your shorts to be. Mark the length with a few pins (don't stab yourself!) and take the jeans off.

2 Lay the jeans down carefully folded in two (so the legs line up). Cut the legs off 5cm below the pins. Cut across both legs at the same time to make sure they're an equal length.

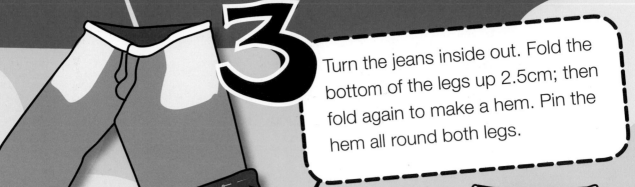

3

Turn the jeans inside out. Fold the bottom of the legs up 2.5cm; then fold again to make a hem. Pin the hem all round both legs.

Tip!
Ironing the hem flat will give a sharper edge and make it easier to sew. You should ask an adult to help you.

4

Thread a needle and knot the thread, then sew around the edge of each hem using backstitch (see page 7). Remove the pins, then turn your shorts the right way out – they're done!

Tip!
Try using contrasting thread – jeans often have yellow or orange stitching. Or decorate your shorts using **appliqué** (see page 26) or bead art (see page 20).

Cool cuffs

Do you ever get chilly wrists? Make your sleeves longer and cosier by adding some snuggly knitted cuffs. This looks good on a coat or denim jacket, and it's a great way to reuse holey old socks and sweaters.

Get the gear

- Garment you want to add cuffs to, e.g. coat or jacket
- Old sweater or pair of socks
- Scissors and tape measure or ruler
- Pins, needles and extra-strong thread

1 Lay your item of clothing with the sleeves pressed flat. You'll need an old sweater that has sleeves the same width, or a pair of worn-out woolly socks that are the right size.

2 Cut off the sleeves or the tops of the socks to the length you want, plus about 2cm. A good length for a cuff is about 6–8cm.

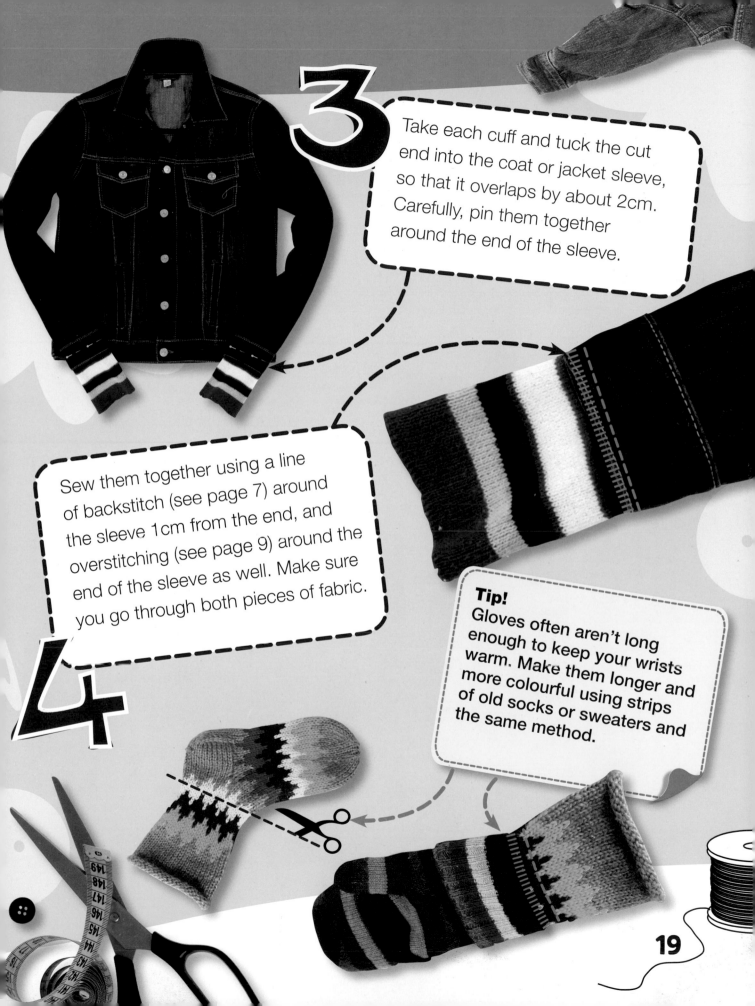

3 Take each cuff and tuck the cut end into the coat or jacket sleeve, so that it overlaps by about 2cm. Carefully, pin them together around the end of the sleeve.

4 Sew them together using a line of backstitch (see page 7) around the sleeve 1cm from the end, and overstitching (see page 9) around the end of the sleeve as well. Make sure you go through both pieces of fabric.

Tip!
Gloves often aren't long enough to keep your wrists warm. Make them longer and more colourful using strips of old socks or sweaters and the same method.

Beads and buttons

Just think of all the billions of beads and buttons in the world! They come in all shapes, colours and designs, and are perfect for customising clothes.

Get the gear!

- Beads and buttons (check first the holes are big enough for a needle)
- Clothes for customising
- Pencil or sewing chalk
- Needles, thread and scissors

Button it

You can brighten up a boring coat, cardie or dress by simply sewing on new buttons. Try a bright contrasting colour, giant buttons, or buttons that are all different.

Button and bead art

Decorate a top, jacket or hat with beads or buttons in a pattern. Start by sketching your design on paper.

1

2

Copy the design lightly onto the garment using a pencil or sewing chalk. Then sew the beads or buttons on to create your design.

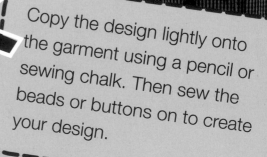

On the edge

Beads look great in a line around a collar or the edge of a pocket. To do this, thread a thin needle with some strong thread and knot the end.

1

2

Thread beads onto the needle and the thread, pushing them together. When you have enough, knot the other end too.

knot

3

Lay the string of beads where you want it, and carefully sew it in place all the way along, using overstitch (see page 9).

Funky footwear

Bored with your trainers? Change them! Canvas shoes are easy to re-colour using fabric paint – as long as they're a light colour to start with. You can add other decorations too.

You'll need...

- Canvas shoes, with laces removed
- Fabric paint
- Cheap art paintbrush
- Newspaper, kitchen roll and rubber gloves
- For decorating, beads, buttons, ribbons, etc. and sewing equipment

1
It's best to paint shoes on the floor or even outdoors, away from carpets and sofas. Spread out the newspaper and wear rubber gloves.

2
Remove the laces before you start painting. Follow the fabric paint instructions and use the brush or applicator provided, or if there isn't one, a small art paintbrush. Put one hand inside the shoe and use the other hand to paint with.

3 You could paint spots, flowers, stripes or an all-over colour. Go slowly to avoid drips and smudges. If you are only painting part of the shoe, do the edges very carefully.

Tip!
Use a strong needle and extra-strong thread to sew through canvas, and check first that they can fit through your beads and buttons.

4 For extra decoration, or to jazz up darker shoes, use the methods from earlier in the book to sew on beads, buttons or ready-made fabric flowers.

Glam sandals

Take a simple pair of flip-flops, slide-on sandals or ballet pumps, and make them glamorous, pretty or super-sparkly.

- Flip-flops, sandals or ballet pumps
- Shiny buttons, beads, fabric flowers or ribbons
- Scissors, sturdy needle and extra-strong thread
- **Thimble**

Stunning sandals

Sandals look great completely covered with beads or buttons. Sew them on one at a time, knotting the thread on the inside of the sandal.

Quick and easy

For a quicker project, sew a row of beads or buttons along an edge, or simply decorate each shoe with a fabric or felt flower (see page 10–11).

Tip!
Whether your sandals are leather, fabric, rubber or plastic, sewing them can be hard work. First use a needle to make the holes, then sew through them. If it's difficult to push the needle through, wear a thimble on your finger.

1 Ankle ties

Add ribbons to sandals to make ankle ties. For each sandal, cut two pieces of ribbon about 60cm long.

2

Sew the ends to the insides of your sandal straps, close to the ankle.

3

To wear, wrap the ribbons around your ankles (or further up the leg if you prefer) and tie in a bow.

Bow ties

For a simpler ribbon effect, just cut a length of ribbon and wrap or tie in a bow around your sandal or flip-flop straps.

Appliqué shapes

Appliqué means making a fabric picture, which you then 'apply' or sew onto something. Create any shape you like, and use it to decorate a T-shirt, hat, bag, cardie or jeans.

Get the gear!

- Paper, pencil and tape measure or ruler
- Scraps of flat, non-stretchy fabric, such as felt, **cord** or printed cotton
- Scissors, pins, needles and thread
- Sewing chalk

1 Start by sketching a shape on paper until you are happy with your design. A good size is about 6–12cm across.

2 Copy your shape onto your chosen fabric in pencil or sewing chalk. Here are a few shape ideas:

Tip!
Try cutting a ready-printed shape out of a fabric that has flowers or other interesting pictures on it.

3 Sew around the shape using backstitch (see page 7), just inside the edge of the shape. If you can use a sewing machine, you can do this on the machine by using a zigzag stitch (turn to the zigzag setting).

4 Carefully cut the shape out, leaving about 0.5cm around the stitching.

5 Pin the shape onto your garment and sew it in place, using overstitch (see page 9) around the edge, plus some backstitch across the middle. You could sew in a swirly or zigzag pattern, or use this stitching to add details. This will hold the shape in place firmly.

Appliqué advanced!

Once you've tried simple appliqué, you can piece together several bits of fabric to make a more complex design. Add beads and buttons to make eyes or other parts of the picture.

Get the gear

- Paper and pencil
- Scraps of flat, non-stretchy fabric, such as felt, cord or printed cotton
- Scissors, pins, needles and thread

1

As before, design your appliqué first. Decide which fabrics to use for which parts, and how many pieces you will need. You may want to join pieces together side by side, like this...

or layer pieces on top of each other like this.

2 Following the method for appliqué on pages 26 and 27, mark your shapes on the fabric, sew around them, then cut them out.

Pin and sew them together using backstitch (see page 7), before attaching them to your garment. **3**

Lastly, add any buttons or beads on top.

4

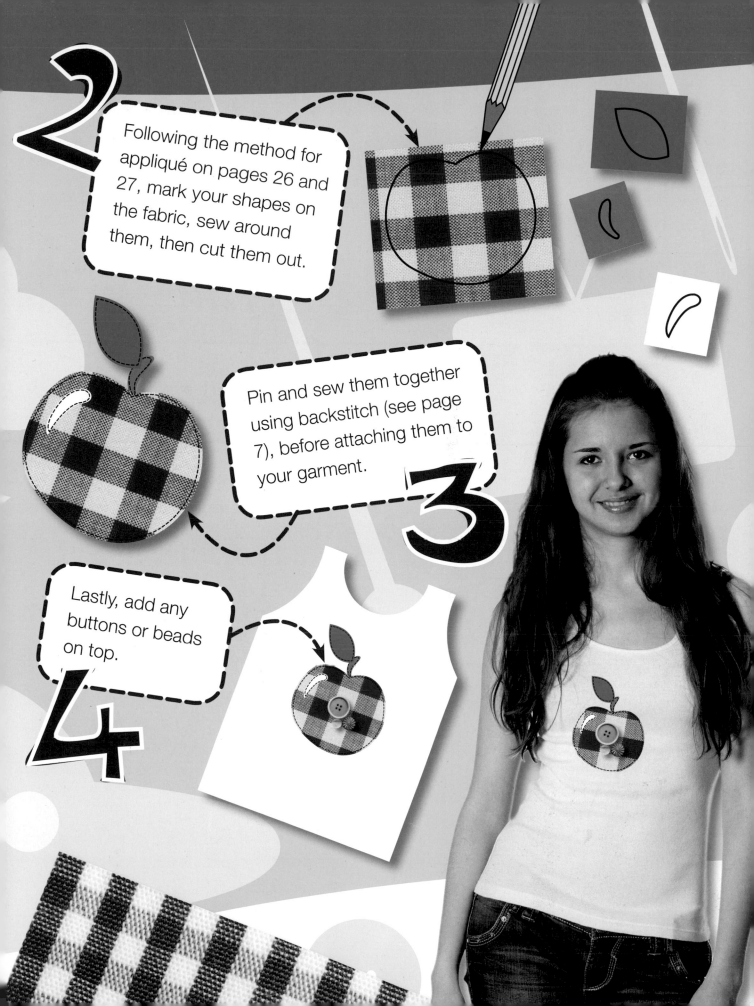

Equipment tips

Beads

Craft shops, toy shops and sewing shops often have beads, and there are also specialist bead shops. You can reuse beads from old or broken jewellery too.

Buttons

You can buy buttons in sewing shops, craft shops and department stores. Also try charity shops and reusing buttons from old clothes.

Embroidery thread

This is often sold in sewing and craft shops or knitting shops, and comes in hundreds of colours. Look for good quality, cotton thread, such as Anchor, which is easy to use and washable.

Fabric

Fabric shops, craft shops and some department stores sell new fabrics by the metre. Check bargain buckets for cheaper **remnants**. IKEA® is great for cheap, funky fabric. Ask friends and family if they have old clothes, bed linen or curtains you could cut up and reuse.

Fabric paint

Craft shops, art shops and toy shops may have this.

Felt

Fabric shops, department stores, craft shops and toy shops often have felt.

Needles

From sewing shops. Look for a variety pack with lots of different sizes.

Old clothes

As well as reusing your own old fabrics, ask family members for anything they don't want any more, and check out charity shops and jumble sales.

Online

There are many fabric and craft shops on the Internet. You may find the following sites useful starting points:
www.handyhippo.co.uk
www.hobbycraft.co.uk
www.myfabrics.co.uk

Pins

From sewing shops. Longer pins with ball-shaped heads are the easiest to use.

Ready-made fabric flowers

From craft and sewing shops.

Ribbons

Sewing and fabric shops usually sell ribbons and trimmings by the metre.

Scissors

The sharper your scissors, the easier they are to work with, but take care when using them. Special sewing, craft or embroidery scissors from a sewing shop are best.

Sequins

You can often find these at craft shops and stationer's.

Sewing machines

This book doesn't show you how to use a sewing machine, but if you have one, you can use it for most of the projects. Follow the machine's instructions, and get an adult to help you. If you want to buy a sewing machine, try a department store or sewing shop.

Tape measure

From sewing, stationery or DIY shops.

Thread

From sewing shops. It's worth buying good quality thread as it's easier to sew with. Use extra-strong thread for sewing through heavy fabrics or shoes.

Glossary

appliqué
A technique used to decorate clothing or other fabric items by attaching fabric shapes.

backstitch
A strong sewing stitch that goes over each part of the fabric twice.

cord (short for corduroy)
A fabric with narrow ridges running along it.

corsage
A small bouquet of flowers worn on your clothes.

customise
To change something to suit you, or add your own designs.

embroidery
Using coloured thread to decorate fabric.

garment
An item of clothing.

gather
To pull fabric together into a bundle or crinkle using a line of stitching.

haberdashery
Ribbons, buttons, pins, needles and other sewing bits and bobs.

hem
The edge of a piece of fabric, folded over and sewn in place to stop it unravelling.

overstitch
A looping sewing stitch for sewing around edges.

remnants
Leftover pieces of fabric.

running stitch
A simple, in-and-out sewing stitch.

sequins
Little shiny or metallic discs with a hole in the middle.

sewing chalk
Sometimes called dressmaker's or tailor's chalk. Special chalk for marking fabric, available from sewing shops.

slogan
A word or phrase.

stash
A place where something is stored – such as your collection of fabrics and sewing stuff!

thimble
A hard cover that you put on your fingertip to help you push a needle through fabric.

Index

Contents

Electric Power!

IT WAS 2.45 PM on 4 September 1882 and a group of New York City's most powerful and influential men were gathered in the offices of J. Pierpoint Morgan, the famous banker and one of the richest men in the world. Tension filled the air. Each of the men stole glances first at their watches, then at one another and finally at the glass bulbs that were arranged on one side of the room. Some of the men had sunk hundreds of thousands of dollars into Mr Edison's latest project, which was the first commercial, electric power supply. They were about to find out if it worked.

BELOW: *The dynamo room of Edison's first electric lighting station, in 1882.*

Meanwhile, just a block or two away at 255 Pearl Street, feverish activity was taking place. This building was home to Edison's electric lighting station and at 3 pm, it was due to light up offices and buildings around the area for the first time. As the moment approached, the engineers realized that there was no more they could do. In the power station and in Mr Morgan's office, all eyes were on the clock as it dragged slowly towards 3 pm. Then the moment came.

The bulbs in Mr Morgan's office flickered. Dimly at first, they began to glow with a strong, steady light. Across the 2 square kilometres surrounding Edison's lighting station, similar bulbs glowed in the offices and factories of his thirty or so other customers. These were the first of many people to experience the wonder of an electric power supply.

Who was Edison?

Thomas A. Edison was one of the greatest inventors the world has ever seen. When Edison was born, the world had no radios, no typewriters, no telephones, no way of recording music, no movies… very few of the inventions we take for granted today. By the time Edison died in 1931, all these things existed, and most of them had grown out of his inventions.

RIGHT: *An early photograph of the Flatiron building in New York City in 1910, just 28 years after Edison first brought electric power to the city.*

'*The point at which I am different from most other inventors is that I have, besides the usual inventor's makeup, a bump of practicality… the sense of the business, money value of an invention.*'

EDISON, DESCRIBING HIS BUSINESS SENSE.

The USA in the Nineteenth Century

EDISON WAS BORN in the USA in 1847. The world at this time was a dynamic, exciting place and towards the end of the nineteenth century, there were few countries more exciting than the USA.

In the north, large factories were springing up as the country's natural resources were used to support manufacturing businesses. Great railways linked both sides of the USA, allowing people and goods to be transported back and forth, and the telegraph allowed people to communicate quickly over long distances. More and more people moved to the cities, where they were able to get jobs. And pushing all this growth forward was a great movement of scientific and technological progress.

BELOW: *Steam trains such as this one allowed people to move westwards in the USA during the nineteenth century.*

The Civil War

In 1861, civil war broke out between the northern and southern states. In many ways, the war mirrored other changes in American life. The increasingly powerful, industrial northern states fought against the largely rural southern states. The North's victory in 1865 reflected the way in which the USA was becoming a world industrial power during the nineteenth century.

The Age of Invention

The nineteenth century gave birth to many of the inventions we associate with modern life, including the telephone, the automobile, electric power and moving pictures. Usually, they resulted from breakthroughs by scientists and engineers. New inventions came thick and fast, though some were not as useful as others. Many crank inventions were advertised alongside ones that would turn out to be truly useful.

ABOVE: *An iron and steel works in Pennsylvania, typical of the industrial northern USA in the mid-19th century.*

BELOW: *One of the many battles of the American Civil War, the Battle of Spotsylvania Court House, May 1864.*

Early Years

Edison's Childhood

Thomas Alva Edison arrived in the world on 11 February 1847, in Milan, a small town near the shore of Lake Erie, in the state of Ohio, USA. His parents were Canadians living in the USA. They had already had six children, but three died before Thomas was born and he was so weak when he was born that his mother was sure he would die too.

When Thomas was seven, his family moved to Port Huron, a larger town on the southern tip of Lake Huron, in the state of Michigan. At school in Port Huron, Thomas had a very hard time. He had trouble with his hearing, and his teacher thought he was backward. Like many teachers of the time, he thought he could beat knowledge into his students. Thomas stayed at the bottom of the class for three months,

ABOVE: *A portrait of Edison as a young boy of about eight.*

BELOW: *A modern-day photo of the house in which Edison was born, in Milan, Ohio.*

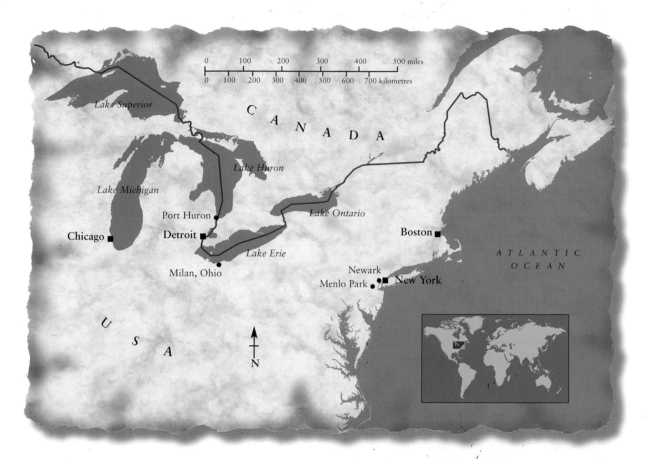

until his mother took him out of school. She had been a schoolteacher herself before marrying Thomas's father, so she decided to teach him at home.

School of Natural Philosophy

Thomas was a keen reader, who read Shakespeare, history books and the Bible. His favourite book was *School of Natural Philosophy*, which suggested simple scientific experiments to do at home. Thomas did them all. He built his own laboratory in his bedroom, but was forced to move it to the basement because of the mess caused by some of his experiments (particularly the explosions!).

IN THEIR OWN WORDS

'My mother taught me how to read good books quickly and correctly, and as this opened up a great world in literature, I have always been very thankful for this early training.'

EDISON IN HIS LATER YEARS, REMEMBERING HIS EARLY EDUCATION.

'That boy is addled [stupid].'

EDISON'S SCHOOLTEACHER, IN 1855.

THE RAILWAY EXPERIMENTER

In 1859, a new railway line opened that linked Port Huron to Detroit. At the age of twelve, Thomas got a job selling newspapers on the trains. He soon sold fruits and sweets as well, to make a bit of extra money.

Thomas set up a laboratory in a corner of an empty luggage car and used his spare time to carry on with his experiments. Unfortunately, one day an experiment got out of hand and the laboratory caught fire. Edison later remembered that the guard, who was burned putting out the fire, boxed his ears as a result!

Read All About It!

In 1861, while Thomas was still working on the trains, the American Civil War broke out. On 6 April 1862, word reached Detroit of a terrible battle being fought at a place

BELOW: *The Battle of Shiloh began on 6 April 1862. By 7 April there would be over 20,000 men lying dead or wounded on the battlefield.*

IN THEIR OWN WORDS

'[A guard] took me by the ears and lifted me. I felt something snap inside my head. My deafness started from that time and has ever since progressed.'

EDISON IN LATER YEARS, DATING THE BEGINNING OF HIS DEAFNESS FROM HIS DAYS AS A NEWSPAPER BOY.

called Shiloh. Thomas sensed that if word of the battle reached people at stations on the way to Port Huron, everyone would want to read about it and he'd sell more newspapers. So he persuaded the Detroit telegraph operator to send a short telegram to each station. Then he raced to the newspaper offices.

Thomas normally only bought a hundred papers, but this time he wanted 1,000 copies. However, he only had enough money to buy 300 so he had to persuade the editor to let him have them on credit. This was quite a gamble for Thomas to take, because he had no real way of paying back the credit if he didn't sell the papers.

Luckily for Thomas, he was right. At the first station, where he normally sold two papers, Thomas sold 200. At the next he sold 300 and decided to put up the price. By the time the train reached home in Port Huron, all the papers were sold and Thomas had made a big profit.

BELOW: *Thomas as a newsboy on the railroad.*

IN THEIR OWN WORDS

'The happiest time in my life was when I was twelve years old. I was just old enough to have a good time in the world, but not old enough to understand any of its troubles.'

EDISON IN 1930, REMEMBERING HIS CHILDHOOD.

THE TELEGRAPH

While working on the Port Huron-to-Detroit line, Edison got to know the telegraph operator, James MacKenzie. Thomas was already interested in telegraphs. He had built a simple version to connect his best friend's house with his own. MacKenzie taught him how to use the type of telegraph found in telegraph offices all round the world.

BELOW: *A telegraph line being constructed beside a railway track in the 1860s. By the end of the nineteenth century, telegraph lines had been put up across large areas of wild country in the USA, connecting communities and sending news of national events.*

Edison the Telegrapher

In the early 1860s, telegraph operators were in great demand, partly because many experienced operators had gone to work for the army in the American Civil War. As a 'tramp' telegrapher, it was possible to travel round the country, working somewhere for a few months, and then moving on somewhere else. To an adventurous young man like Edison, the chance was too good to miss. In 1863, at the age of sixteen, he decided to become a tramp telegrapher.

Edison never stopped experimenting. As a telegraph operator, he liked the night shift best, which left the day free for his experiments. The night shift helped develop one of his first inventions. Night operators were supposed to send a signal every half-hour to show that they were awake. Edison, tired from a hard day's inventing, needed to sleep, so he created a device that sent the signal automatically. It worked perfectly, until his bosses found out and he got the sack.

IN THEIR OWN WORDS

'I built a telegraph wire between our houses… The wire was that used for suspending stove pipes, the insulators were small bottles pegged on ten-penny nails driven into trees. It worked fine.'

EDISON REMEMBERING THE TELEGRAPH SYSTEM HE MADE BETWEEN HIS FRIEND'S HOME AND HIS OWN.

THE TELEGRAPH

Telegraphs used electric currents sent along a wire to send messages from place to place. Telegraph operators tapped a lever with their hand to start the current. At the other end, the current was heard as a click. Pressing the lever down for a longer time made a long click, whereas a short press made a short click. The sender sent a message using the Morse code, where the clicks stood for letters of the alphabet.

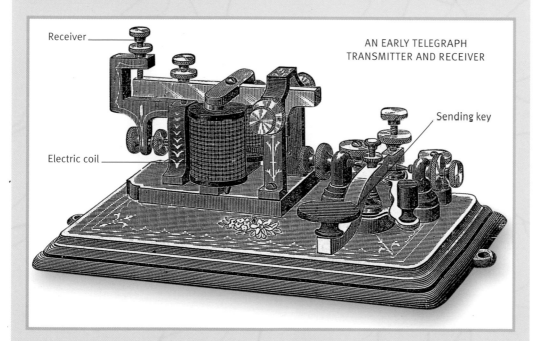

Receiver

Electric coil

Sending key

AN EARLY TELEGRAPH TRANSMITTER AND RECEIVER

THE MOVE TO BOSTON

In 1868, after four years as a tramp telegrapher, 21-year-old Edison arrived in Boston and got a job with the Western Union Telegraph Company. On his first day, the other telegraph operators looked at the scruffy young man and thought he must be a young, inexperienced operator who needed to learn how quickly things were done in the big city. They set him up to receive messages from a press operator in New York. Press operators were the fastest in the business and Edison knew it, but he didn't say a word. He was a first-class operator himself.

The messages started to come over the wire at an alarming speed, but Edison kept up. Finally, in desperation, the operator at the other end started using abbreviations. Edison interrupted him and cheekily sent back the message: 'You seem to be tired. Suppose you send a little while with

BELOW: *State Street in Boston, in about 1840. By the time Edison arrived in 1868, Boston had grown into a bigger, much busier city.*

FIRST INVENTIONS

One of Edison's first inventions was an electronic vote counter for the US Congress. The counter worked perfectly, but there was one problem – Congress didn't want to buy it. Edison learned a hard lesson: it's no good inventing things that no one wants, because they don't make any money.

Another invention was much more successful: Edison's 'stock ticker.' This was a telegraph-based device that transmitted news of changes in the values of stocks and shares. The news was printed out on long strips of paper, called 'ticker tape'. This information was valuable to banks and other financial groups, who were willing to pay for it.

EDISON'S FIRST STOCK TICKER

Ticker tape shows prices

your other foot?' The room exploded with laughter. Edison had suggested the operator was using his foot to tap out the messages instead of his hand.

Trouble

In the middle of the nineteenth century, Boston was the centre of the USA's scientific community. When he wasn't working at the Western Union, Edison was working on his experiments in the workshop of Charles Williams's Electrical Shop on Court Street. But Edison didn't stay in Boston long. Later in 1868, he got into trouble with his superiors at Western Union by writing down the messages in tiny letters which were hard to read. When told to write bigger, Edison responded by writing all his messages in very large letters. Immediately demoted, Edison walked out.

IN THEIR OWN WORDS

'T.A. Edison has resigned his [job] at the Western Union office, Boston, and will devote his time to bringing out inventions.'

A NOTICE IN *THE TELEGRAPHER* A NEWSPAPER FOR TELEGRAPHERS, IN JANUARY 1869.

TO NEW YORK

In 1869, Edison moved to New York City. He arrived with nothing, not even a place to stay, but he was quickly back in the inventing business. Soon after he arrived, Edison met up with Franklin Pope, who worked for the Gold Indicator Company. This company had invented the gold indicator, the very first stock ticker, which showed the changing prices for buying and selling gold. One day at Pope's office, the gold indicator broke down. There was a panic – no one knew what to do – until Edison calmly fixed the machine within two hours.

BELOW: *New York City's Broadway, in 1887. By this time it was (and still is) one of the USA's most popular shopping streets.*

The New York office of the Western Union Telegraph Company asked Edison to sort out a problem with its transmitting equipment. Edison found a solution fairly quickly and Western Union asked to buy the device he had invented. Edison visited their offices. He wanted $5,000, but hardly dared to ask for so much money. While Edison hesitated, the Western Union representative offered $40,000 for the device. 'This caused me to come as near to fainting as I ever got,' Edison later said.

IN THEIR OWN WORDS

'People here come and buy without your soliciting [trying].'

EDISON, WRITING ABOUT NEW YORK TO A FRIEND BACK IN BOSTON.

A New Laboratory

Edison used his windfall to start a laboratory and factory in Newark, New Jersey, producing stock tickers and other equipment. In 1871, on Christmas Day, he married Mary Stillwell, whom he had met earlier that year, when she came to work at the factory. Some stories say that after the wedding, Edison went back to his laboratory and stayed there until midnight, to finish an experiment he had started.

The 'Invention Factory'

In 1876 Edison moved again, to the tiny settlement of Menlo Park, New Jersey. By this time, he and Mary had a four-year-old daughter, Marion. In Menlo Park, Edison gathered together skilled craftspeople who would be able to make parts for his inventions. Their aim was to bring out an invention every ten days and what Edison called a 'big trick' every six months.

King of the Patents

Edison wasn't just a great inventor. He was also good at making sure he got the credit (and the profit) for his inventions. In his lifetime, Edison took out 1,093 patents on new ideas.

RIGHT: *Mary Stillwell in about 1871, the year of her marriage to Edison.*

The Great Inventions

*'I am so deaf
that I am
debarred
from hearing
all the finer
articulations [words], and
have to depend on the
judgement of others.'*

EDISON TELLING A JOURNALIST ABOUT
HIS HEARING DIFFICULTIES IN 1877.

BELOW: *Alexander Graham Bell
is the first to use the New York–
Chicago telephone link in 1892.*

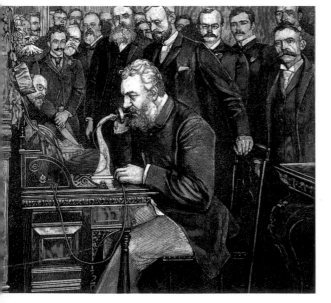

The Telephone

In 1876, news reached the world that a Scotsman named Alexander Graham Bell had succeeded in transmitting the human voice down a wire. The first telephone had been created. Western Union immediately asked Edison to see if he could improve on the device, which wasn't able to work over long distances.

On the face of it, Western Union might have seemed crazy to ask Edison to improve on the telephone. Edison, after all, was practically deaf by now and could barely hear normal conversations. He was only able to go to the theatre (one of his favourite pastimes) if he could get front-row seats, and his assistants quite often had to bellow at him to be heard. Was this really the right man to improve a device that required its users to listen to words transported down a wire?

Nonetheless, the Western Union president, William Orton, thought Edison was the right man for the job. He called Edison 'probably the best electro-mechanician in the country.' There was also the fact that by asking Edison to improve the telephone, Western Union was enlisting the help not just of Edison, but also his team of assistants. Menlo Park was the largest private laboratory in the USA, and Edison had hired some very clever people to work there. All of them would help solve the problem of the telephone.

The very first telephones had several problems. They used the same device for sending and receiving, so you could not listen if you were talking. Also, the signal they sent down the wire was weak and would not carry far. It was these areas that Edison hoped to improve.

LEFT: *Edison (middle-row, centre) and his chief assistants from the Menlo Park laboratory.*

HOW BELL'S TELEPHONE WORKED

The human voice produces vibrations in the air, which produce similar vibrations in a thin sheet, or diaphragm, of iron. In Bell's telephone, a diaphragm is placed near a magnet. The magnet has a coil of wire wound around it. In the sending instrument, or transmitter, the diaphragm vibrates in response to the voice and an electric signal is produced in the coil of wire. The signal travels to the receiving telephone and varies the magnetism, so that the diaphragm there vibrates in the same way, reproducing the original sound.

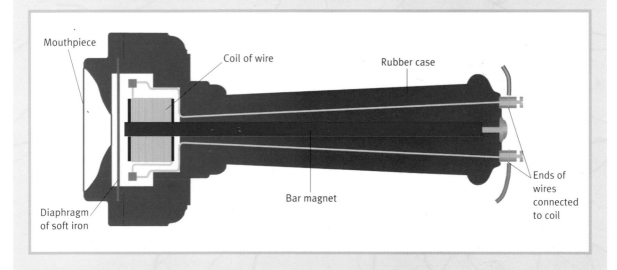

Mouthpiece
Coil of wire
Rubber case
Bar magnet
Ends of wires connected to coil
Diaphragm of soft iron

EDISON'S TELEPHONE

Edison used to say that being deaf was an excellent way of making sure his new telephone finally worked. If he could hear it, it must be loud and clear! The Menlo Park team worked long hours trying to improve the telephone. Often Edison didn't go home until breakfast time, and his employees were expected to work just as hard. He once locked the doors and told them that they couldn't leave until the job was finished! Edison's wife, Mary, found this a difficult time. There were few people in Menlo Park apart from the workers and she felt so scared without her husband in the house that she slept with a pistol under her pillow.

By 1877, at the age of thirty, Edison was ready to demonstrate his new, improved telephone. He and his assistants had made two main improvements to Bell's original design. Since the transmitter was separated from the receiver, it became possible to interrupt someone at the other end of the line if one caller didn't agree with what the other was saying! The new telephone could be also be used over greater distances. Many of the telephones we use today work on exactly the same principles as Edison's improved version.

LEFT: *An illustration of the Menlo Park laboratories.*

Despite his success with the telephone, Edison, though famous in the scientific community, was still not a household name. The invention that would make him truly famous was just around the corner, and the story starts (on the next page) with a child's toy.

HOW EDISON'S TELEPHONE WORKED

Edison's telephone had the same receiver as Bell's, but a different sending instrument, or transmitter. In Bell's telephone, all the power came from the voice of a person speaking. In Edison's telephone, the power came from a battery, which produced an electric current.

The new transmitter was much more effective in turning voice vibrations into electric pulses. A diaphragm inside the transmitter formed the side of a box containing carbon granules. When the diaphragm vibrated, the electrical resistance between the granules varied, changing the current produced by the battery.

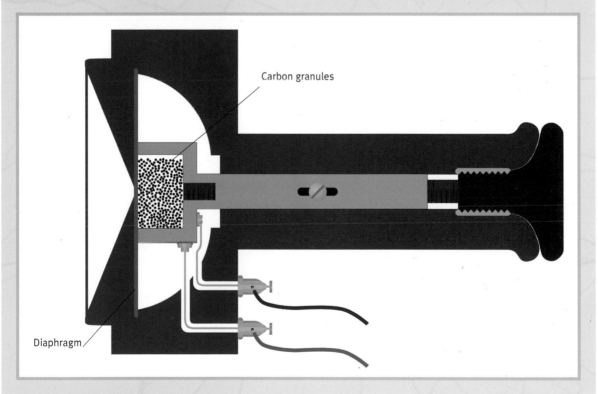

Carbon granules

Diaphragm

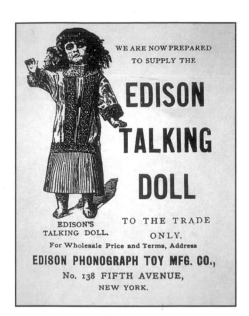

ABOVE: *An advertisement for the Edison Talking Doll.*

BELOW: *From right to left, Edison, Charles Batchelor and Uriah Painter in 1878, when they went to Washington to demonstrate the phonograph.*

THE PHONOGRAPH

While working on the design for the telephone, Edison made a toy for his daughter, Marion. It used a carbon diaphragm, like the ones used in telephones, to respond to the vibrations of a human voice. The movement of the diaphragm provided electrical power for a model of a man sawing wood. Edison began to think that perhaps if the movement of the diaphragm could be recorded in some way, it might be possible to make the diaphragm reproduce the original sound using the same movement.

Soon, Edison had a working model of his 'phonograph', or 'sound writer'. The device was named after the Ancient Greek words *phonos*, meaning 'sound', and *graph*, meaning 'writing'. Edison demonstrated it to his assistants by playing them a recording of himself reciting the child's nursery rhyme 'Mary Had A Little Lamb'. His assistants were amazed, and the rest of the USA – indeed, the rest of the world – was soon to follow.

'The Wizard of Menlo Park'

The phonograph quickly caught the public's attention. Exhibitions and demonstrations were organized, at which people paid 25c to hear the phonograph in action. A novelty model was sold for $30, which was a huge amount in those days. This was quickly withdrawn because Edison planned to charge even more for his 'standard' version and didn't want people to buy the cheaper one. The world was gripped by Edison-mania: in Europe and America, people were desperate to find out more about the man the press called 'The Wizard of Menlo Park'. Edison even went to Washington to demonstrate his phonograph to President Hayes.

HOW THE PHONOGRAPH WORKED

The phonograph had a diaphragm behind a mouthpiece. Sound made the diaphragm vibrate, which moved a needle attached to its centre. The needle made dents on a drum covered with tin foil. When the needle was passed back over the dents, the diaphragm recreated the original sound. It was such a simple idea that Alexander Graham Bell, the inventor of the telephone, said it was 'a most astonishing thing to me that I could possibly have let this invention slip through my fingers.'

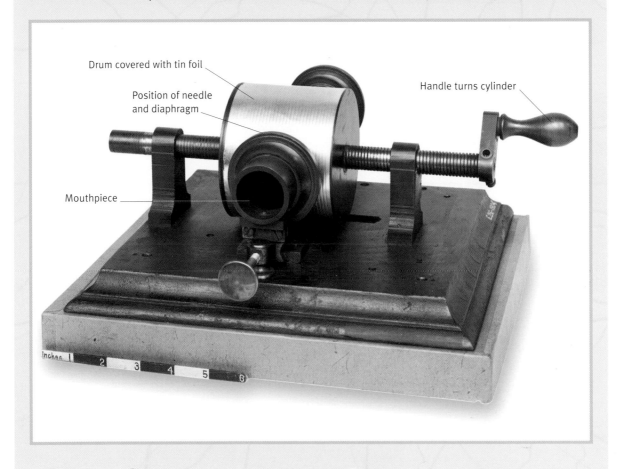

Drum covered with tin foil

Position of needle and diaphragm

Handle turns cylinder

Mouthpiece

Tired out, in 1878 Edison took his first holiday since his honeymoon in 1871. He travelled to Wyoming to see the total eclipse of the sun in July, then on to San Francisco, Yosemite and then Nevada. But, in the back of his mind, Edison was probably already thinking about his next big project: the light bulb.

ELECTRIC LIGHT

In the nineteenth century, the gas companies were among the most powerful in the USA. Apart from oil and candles, they were the main source of lighting to homes and businesses in America's cities. Edison saw that if he could challenge the gas companies, he might become a very wealthy man.

He formed the Edison Electric Company with the aim of supplying electric light instead. The announcement that Edison planned to compete with the gas companies sparked

RIGHT: *An artist's impression of assistants at Menlo Park, trying to carbonize a filament for an electric light bulb.*

a stockmarket crash. In late 1878, the value of shares in the gas companies suddenly dropped by 25-30 per cent, as investors raced to get rid of them before Edison put the gas companies out of business.

To produce electric light, the main problem facing Edison was to find a suitable material for the filament. After trying thousands of substances, he found that he could make a good filament by carbonizing a fibre from a particular variety of bamboo. Edison also had to set up a glass-blowing factory to produce the light bulbs, and make a machine that could create a vacuum inside them.

Finally, Edison was able to make a light bulb that lasted long enough to be useful. By Christmas of 1878, crowds from across the USA were flocking to Menlo Park. Edison's laboratory and home were lit up like beacons using electric light bulbs, or 'incandescent lamps' as they were also called.

HOW THE LIGHT BULB WORKED

Early light bulbs were very like those we use today. They were made up of a sealed glass bulb with a vacuum inside. Inside the bulb was a thin filament, which would heat up and glow when electricity passed through it, providing light.

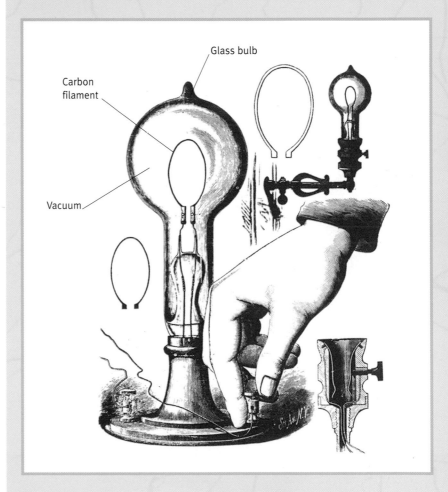

Glass bulb

Carbon filament

Vacuum

ELECTRIC POWER

Having created the light bulb, Edison now had to find a way of producing electric power. By the summer of 1879, Edison and his team had invented a generator that turned steam into electricity far more efficiently than any other. Because of its strange shape they called it 'Long-legged Mary-Anne'.

Work continued on other uses of electric power. In May 1880, Edison demonstrated an electric train in the grounds of Menlo Park. Guests had to hang on tight as the train whizzed over bumps and through turns at 40 kilometres per hour, but the return journey wasn't half as exciting. The train broke down and the guests had to push it home.

Edison Electric Light Company

In 1880 Edison bought two buildings on Pearl Street in Lower Manhattan, New York, to be the base for the Edison Electric Light Company. By the spring of 1881, he and his family had moved from Menlo Park to a rented house on Gramercy Lane, so that Edison could be nearer to his newest business. He was convinced it was going to be a great success.

In 1882, the Edison Electric Light Company began to supply power to nearby businesses. This early power could only be supplied within a 4-kilometre radius. Even so, within a short time electric power stations had sprung up across the USA. (See pages 4–5 for details about the day the lights were first switched on.)

LEFT: *Edison's super-efficient generator, the 'Long-legged Mary-Anne', was at the heart of his success. It converted more energy into electricity than other dynamos at the time.*

PARALLEL CIRCUITS

Edison's wiring for his new electricity-supply business used parallel circuits, where each lamp only receives a fraction of the total current. This meant that it was possible for one part of the circuit to be turned off without stopping the electricity supply to all the other parts.

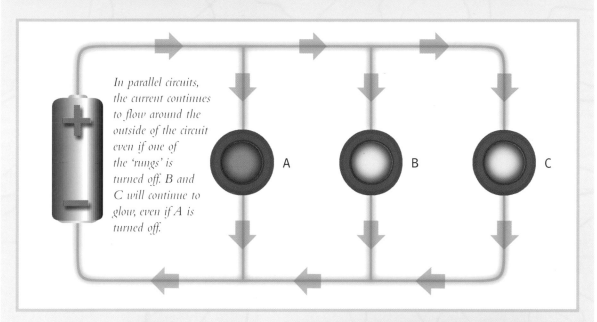

In parallel circuits, the current continues to flow around the outside of the circuit even if one of the 'rungs' is turned off. B and C will continue to glow, even if A is turned off.

A   B   C

IN THEIR OWN WORDS

'I have accomplished all that I promised.'

EDISON TO REPORTERS AFTER HIS
PEARL STREET POWER STATION BEGAN
WORK ON 4 SEPTEMBER 1882.

RIGHT: *Edison driving the electric train that ran in the grounds of his Menlo Park laboratory.*

Inventor and Businessman

Mary Edison Dies

By 1884, Edison was a famous inventor and a wealthy man with a thriving business. Then tragedy struck. His wife Mary caught typhoid and died. Edison was racked with grief. He couldn't bear to go back to his house in Menlo Park, so the family moved permanently into an apartment on East 18th Street in Lower Manhattan.

Mina Miller

The next summer, Edison met 20-year-old Mina Miller. He was captivated. Mina was beautiful and lively, as well as being a college graduate (which was unusual for a woman at that time). Edison taught Mina the Morse code so that they could speak to each other privately even when there were other people around. During a carriage ride one day, he tapped out the question 'Will you marry me?' on her hand. A breathless wait followed, until she tapped back a message on his hand: 'Yes.' For the rest of their lives, the two communicated in Morse when they wanted to hold private conversations.

RIGHT: *Mina Miller, who was Edison's second wife.*

IN THEIR OWN WORDS

'[He was] shaking with grief, weeping and sobbing so he could hardly tell me my mother had died in the night.'

EDISON'S DAUGHTER MARION, REMEMBERING HER FATHER THE MORNING AFTER HER MOTHER HAD DIED.

Mina tapped out other people's words on her husband's hand so that he could 'hear' what was being said.

West Orange

In 1886, soon after the Edisons returned from their honeymoon, there was a dispute between the managers and workers at the Edison Machine Works, Edison's factory in New York City. As a result, the whole business was moved to Schenectady, in New York state. Only some of the workers kept their jobs.

When they returned from their honeymoon, the Edisons bought a house in West Orange, New Jersey. Edison began work on a new laboratory, which was to be ten times the size of the old Menlo Park 'invention factory'. Once the new laboratory opened, Edison began to oversee a large number of projects at the same time. He had gone from being a full-time inventor to being the head of a large research and development company.

Legal Battles

In 1883, Edison began the first of many legal battles with people whom he felt had copied his inventions. Over the course of his career he would spend over $2 million on such courtroom disputes.

RIGHT: *Edison in his new laboratory.*

'I am experimenting upon an instrument which does for the eye what the phonograph does for the ear, which is the recording and reproduction of things in motion.'

EDISON IN 1888.

BELOW: *Edison looking at film that was first developed in the 1880s.*

MOVING PICTURES

In 1888, Edison was visited by a British photographer called Eadweard Muybridge, who wanted to set a sequence of pictures to the accompaniment of phonograph sound. The project didn't work, but it gave Edison the idea of combining his phonograph technology with film. Edison and his assistant, William Dickson, coated a phonograph-type cylinder in light-sensitive film, then put it inside a camera case. Each time a picture was taken of a moving object, the cylinder was turned slightly. Then another picture was taken. Once the film was processed and the sequence of pictures run through a viewer, the audience could see motion.

At about this time, George Eastman invented a new celluloid film that was far less bulky than anything that had been seen before. In 1889, Edison ordered some Eastman film to be cut up into long strips. William Dickson worked out a way of running the film through a camera by turning a crank. Between them the two men had invented the 'kinetograph', along with a viewer, the 'kinetoscope'.

Edison began making movies in the 'Black Maria', a black-painted building in West Orange. The building was built on tracks so that it could follow the sunlight, to make filming easier. His first movie with a plot was *The Great Train Robbery*. In the end, over 2,000 films were made in the Black Maria. Among them were the first talking motion pictures and the first colour movie (made by hand-painting each frame of the film).

Audiences reacted with panic to the first movies. Not knowing what they were seeing, people watching a film in which a wave broke towards the camera fled from the cinema. They thought the wave was actually coming out of the wall to drown them.

IN THEIR OWN WORDS

'My plan was to synchronize the camera and the phonograph so as to record sounds when the pictures were made, and reproduce the two in harmony... We had the first of the so-called "talking pictures" in our laboratory thirty years ago.'

EDISON SPEAKING IN 1925.

The Twentieth Century

Mining

For a time, as the nineteenth century drew to a close, it seemed that Edison's touch had deserted him. He became involved in a project to extract iron ore from low-grade deposits in the New Jersey mountains. Iron ore was the basis of much US manufacturing industry. If it could be made to work, the new technology would allow iron ore to be mined close to home, instead of having to be brought in from elsewhere.

BELOW: *Edison (standing on the left) on a camping trip in 1918 with some of the most influential men in the USA. From the left, they are Edison, Harvey Firestone Jr, John Burroughs, Henry Ford, Harvey Firestone and (seated below), RJH de Loach.*

'Well, it's all gone, but we had a hell of a good time spending it.'

EDISON, AFTER THE FAILURE OF THE IRON-ORE PROJECT.

LEFT: *Edison always found it easy to relax away from 'society', either at the mines or on camping trips.*

Edison loved the mining culture. He spent weeks up in the hills with his sleeves rolled up and a dirty face, camping with the mining men and working on his ideas. But just as the technology was starting to work, high-grade iron-ore deposits were discovered near Lake Superior, in the Midwest of the USA. It was no longer worth mining the low-grade deposits and the mining company went bust. With it went $2 million of Edison's money.

Concrete

Edison's next big project used some of the technology from his mining experiences. He set up a cement works, which used a giant kiln to bake cement blocks. Edison thought that they could be used to build roads or even houses, but the business never became as successful as he hoped.

CARS AND THE ELECTRIC STORAGE BATTERY

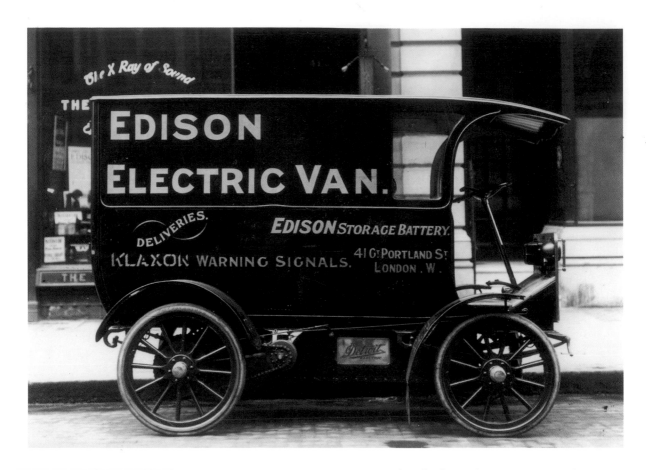

IN THEIR OWN WORDS

'I do not know how long it would take to wear out one of the batteries, for we have not been able to exhaust the possibilities of one of them. But I feel sure one will last longer than four or five automobiles.'

EDISON TALKING TO THE PRESS ABOUT HIS NEW ELECTRIC STORAGE BATTERY IN 1903.

ABOVE: *Edison's electric battery was popular for use in vans such as this one because it was so tough.*

After the failure of the mining project, Edison thought he might succeed with the car industry. He set himself a simple target: to make an electric battery that would power a car for 160 kilometres at 40 kilometres per hour. It took years, but in 1903 Edison unveiled an electric storage battery, which he claimed was far superior to any other. It also turned out to be more expensive.

The manufacture and sale of the Edison battery only began in 1910. Several firms brought out electric cars and trucks that used the battery, and because it lasted for so long, it was especially popular for trucks travelling long distances. However, other firms had also brought out electric batteries and Edison's struggled to gain popularity. But the real problem was created by Edison's friend, Henry Ford. In 1908, Ford had brought out his petrol-driven Model T car. It was by far the cheapest car that had yet been made, and was hugely popular. Most importantly, it established the idea that cars were driven by petrol, not electricity, in the American public mind.

Edison set his mind to finding other uses for his battery. Soon it was being sold for use in railroad signals, ships and submarines, radios, miners' lamps and as a back-up power source for businesses and isolated homes. The Edison Storage Battery Company was earning $25,000 a month by 1912, and continued to do well for many more years.

IN THEIR OWN WORDS

'The horse is doomed. The horseless vehicle is the coming wonder.'

EDISON IN 1895.

BELOW: *Henry Ford and his son in a Model T car. The Model T was so popular that electric cars did not sell in large enough quantities to be profitable.*

THE WINTER HOME

By 1900, Edison no longer worked non-stop all year round. He often came home for meals on time and, starting in 1901, he and Mina spent every winter in a house he had built in Fort Myers, Florida. Of course Edison had a laboratory there too, so that he could carry on with his experiments. There was also a botanical garden filled with over 300 plants from around the world, many of which were used in Edison's experiments.

BELOW: *Edison with George Eastman, who developed strip film for Edison's kinetoscope in 1888.*

The house in Florida was originally one of two. The other house belonged to Edison's childhood friend Ezra Gilliand. But Gilliand only stayed for a year after the homes were built in 1884. After he helped someone defeat Edison in a patent dispute, Edison bought him out and converted the two homes into one.

The house was called Seminole Lodge and, like everything Edison was involved with, it was carefully designed. The veranda was 4 metres wide and all the rooms had high ceilings. A breeze from the river flowed through the open veranda doors and kept the house cool, while the wide veranda kept the house dry even during afternoon showers.

After Mina's death in 1947, Seminole Lodge became a museum and memorial to Edison. All the furnishings and decorations are kept just as they were when Edison and Mina lived there. Every year over 320,000 visitors come to see the house and gardens, as well as the holiday home of Henry Ford, which is next door to Seminole Lodge.

IN THEIR OWN WORDS

'He invents all the while, even in his dreams.'

MINA EDISON, DESCRIBING HER HUSBAND.

BELOW: *Edison tests an improved version of his original phonograph, in his laboratory at Seminole Lodge, in 1900.*

EDISON'S CHILDREN

Edison had six children in all: three (Marion, Tom and William) from his first marriage to Mary, and three more with Mina (Madeleine, Charles and Theodore). After his unsuccessful mining venture, Edison was less busy with experiments and business, and he spent more time with his second family than he had with his first. Theodore eventually worked for his father for a while before leaving to set up his own successful research and development company, called Calibron. Charles also became a respected businessman, and at one time was president of Edison's company before becoming governor of New Jersey.

BELOW: *Thomas Edison Jr (right), Edison's eldest son and second child, who he nicknamed 'Dash' (his first child, Mary, was nicknamed 'Dot'). On the left is William, Edison's third child.*

IN THEIR OWN WORDS

'I see no reason whatever why I should support my son; he has done me no honour and has brought the flush of shame to my cheeks many times… Let [Tom] earn his money like I did. I will continue to send the monthly installment until such time as I think best, but in no case will I loan any more money or increase the monthly amount.'

EDISON REPLYING TO HIS DAUGHTER-IN-LAW'S REQUEST THAT HE GIVE TOM MORE MONEY.

Edison did not have good relationships with his older children. He fell out with his daughter Marion, who felt hurt when she became ill in Europe and received just 'two short letters' from home during her seven-week recovery. Marion returned from Europe in 1892, but soon left and went back to Europe for the second time, eventually marrying a German army officer, Oscar Oeser. Marion lived in Europe until her marriage failed, after the First World War.

Tom in particular had a difficult relationship with his father. He once said that Edison had 'no more right to be a father than a child of six.' The two battled for years over the right to use the Edison name in business. Edison felt his son was ruining his reputation by bringing out badly designed products labelled 'Edison', and threatened court action. William also fell out with his father over use of the family name when he tried to bring out an 'Edison Spark Plug' for cars. Their quarrel, though, was patched up relatively quickly.

ABOVE: *Edison on his seventy-seventh birthday. On Edison's right is his second wife, Mina, with whom he had three more children (Madeleine, Charles and Theodore).*

THE MAN WHO INVENTED THE FUTURE

In 1913, an article on Edison described him as 'this big, smiling, white-haired, blue-eyed, 66-year-old boy.' He had lost none of his enthusiasm, but Edison never again came up with a 'big trick'. The great age of invention was over. New discoveries were made, but they never came heaped one upon the other in the way they did during Edison's heyday.

Edison was awarded the Congressional Gold Medal in 1928, in recognition of inventions that 'revolutionized civilization.' In 1929, he attended a banquet given by President Hoover to celebrate the fiftieth birthday of the light bulb. In the midst of the celebrations, Edison collapsed. After this, he became increasingly unwell.

ABOVE: *This photo, taken on Edison's eighty-second birthday, shows him with (left to right) President Hoover, Henry Ford and (right) Harvey Firestone. By now Edison was one of the most famous people in the world.*

All his life, Edison had followed the teachings of a man named Cornaro, who thought that people ate far more food than they really needed. For most of his life Edison's daily food was one slice of toast, two glasses of milk, one tablespoon of cooked oats, one tablespoon of chopped spinach, one sardine and four biscuits. He believed that this combination of foods was the one that suited his stomach best. In his last years Edison ate just one orange and drank seven glasses of milk each day. By 1931 Edison was suffering from diabetes and a stomach ulcer and, in October, he died.

Soon after Edison's death, President Hoover announced that mourners throughout the USA should turn out their electric lights for one minute. On the evening of 21 October 1931, a wave of darkness swept across the country. The lights went out across the greatest nation in the world, as a mark of respect for, as many newspapers claimed at the time, 'the man who invented the future'.

IN THEIR OWN WORDS

'We are inclined to regard him as one of the wonders of the world.'

FROM THE JOURNAL, *Scientific American*, 1878.

LEFT: *Henry Ford talking to Edison, who was almost completely deaf by this time, at the fiftieth anniversary party for Edison's electric light bulb in 1929.*

The Legacy of Edison

THOMAS ALVA EDISON was one of the most remarkable people ever to have lived. There are very few people who can truly be said to have changed the world. Most of them, for example Hitler, made the world a worse place for everyone who came into contact with them. Edison made the world a better place for vast numbers of people. He worked on many thousands of ideas throughout his life, and a list of just a few of them is awe-inspiring:

BELOW: *Every night, the New York City skyline and thousands of other cities are a blaze of colour – and it was Edison who first lit up New York.*

- The adaptations made to the telephone by Edison are still in use today, well over 100 years later. He changed the telephone into a device that allowed people to talk with each other across long distances.

- Edison was one of the first people to bring reliable, safe light and power to homes and businesses in the form of electricity. It's almost impossible now to imagine a world without electricity: there would no flicking a switch to turn on a light, no refrigerated food, no plug-in stereos, computer games or kettles.

- Edison made the first breakthroughs in sound recording, inventing the first device that allowed sound to be recorded and played back. Without this we would have no music from record, CD and cassette players, and no sound from televisions or cinemas.

- The first commercial movies were made in Edison's laboratories. Imagine a world without Hollywood films and all the other movies that are made each year.

Of course, Edison didn't do all the work on all these things alone. He had helpers in his laboratories, and often the ideas had been worked on before by someone else, or were worked on later by other people. But these others might only have worked on one part of, for example, the challenge of electricity. Only Edison was involved in everything; only Edison could really claim to have guided the world into the future.

BELOW: *A statue of Edison as a young man in Port Huron.*

Timeline

1831

Faraday's Law of Electrical Induction improves the world's understanding of how electricity works.

1847

11 FEBRUARY: Thomas Alva Edison born in Milan, Ohio.

1848

Revolutions sweep across Europe, especially France, Italy, Germany and the Austro-Hungarian Empire. Gold is discovered in California.

1854

The Edison family moves to Port Huron, Michigan.

1855

Thomas attends school for three months before his mother starts to teach him at home.

1859

Twelve-year-old Edison starts working on the Port Huron-Detroit railway as a newspaper boy.
17 OCTOBER: John Brown seizes government weapons at Harper's Ferry, Virginia, to try and start a slave uprising.
First oil well in Pennsylvania.
Charles Darwin's *The Origin of the Species through Natural Selection* is published.

1860

Lincoln is elected US President.

1861–65

American Civil War.

1861

21 JULY: Southern General Robert E. Lee is victorious at the First Battle of Bull Run.

1862

6-7 APRIL: Battle of Shiloh. Edison uses the telegraph to send word of the battle ahead, to sell extra newspapers.
27-30 AUGUST: General Lee wins the Second Battle of Bull Run.

1863

Edison becomes a telegrapher, and spends the next few years moving from place to place.
1 JANUARY: President Lincoln proclaims the emancipation of slaves in the USA.
1-4 MAY: General Lee wins the Battle of Chancellorsville.
1-3 JULY: Confederate army is defeated at the Battle of Gettysburg.

1865

9 APRIL: General Lee surrenders to Union General Grant, at Appomatox Courthouse.
14 APRIL: President Lincoln is assassinated in Washington DC.

1866

Ku Klux Klan formed.

1868

Edison arrives in Boston. He works for Western Union Telegraph Company and registers his first patent, on his electronic vote recorder.

1869

JANUARY: Edison becomes a freelance inventor. He patents his improvements to the stock ticker.
OCTOBER: Edison and Franklin Pope set up a partnership, which soon dissolves. Wyoming state introduces women's suffrage (the right to vote).

1870–71

War between France and Prussia.

1871

Germany united as one country for the first time.

1871

Edison establishes manufacturing shop in New Jersey.
DECEMBER: marries Mary Stillwell.

1876

Edison sets up a new laboratory in Menlo Park, New Jersey, which is christened 'the invention factory'.
MARCH: Alexander Graham Bell patents his telephone.

1877

Edison improves on Bell's telephone.
DECEMBER: Edison invents the phonograph.

1878

Work starts on the electric
light system.

1879

OCTOBER: Carbonized string is
used as a filament for an
electric light bulb.

1880

Electric railway in Menlo Park
is demonstrated.

1881

Edison rents a house
in Manhattan.

1882

4 SEPTEMBER: Power is switched
on at the Pearl Street electric
station of the Edison Electric
Light Company.

1884

Edison's wife Mary dies.

1885

Karl Benz and Gottlieb Daimler
produce the first motor cars
in Germany.

1886

Edison marries Mina Miller,
and moves to West Orange,
New Jersey.
Slavery is abolished in Cuba.

1887

Edison builds a laboratory ten
times the size of Menlo Park
at West Orange.

1888

Edison begins work on his
project to extract iron ore from
low-grade deposits in the
New Jersey hills.
Slavery is abolished in Brazil.

1891

The kinetoscope is patented.

1893

Recession in the USA.

1898

Spanish-American War. US gains
Cuba, Puerto Rica, Guam and
the Philippines.

1899

Edison begins work on the
electric storage battery for
cars and trucks.

1900

Edison, having spent about $2
million, finally abandons his
iron-ore project.

1902

Edison sets up a successful cement
works. Ideas on road-building
and house-building projects
came from
the cement
business, but
were not a
success.

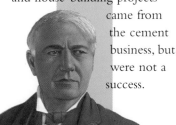

1910

Edison's first commercial electrical
storage battery is released for sale.

1912

Work starts on an electric
self-starter for Henry Ford's
Model T car.

1913

The Ford Company begins mass
production of car parts on an
assembly line.

1914–18

First World War rages across
Europe and other parts of the
world. The USA joins the war
in 1917. Edison spends much
of the war working on
US Navy projects.

1917

Revolution in Russia overthrows
Tsar; Lenin declares a
communist regime.

1927

Edison sets up a project in Florida
to research home-grown
sources of rubber.

1929

NOVEMBER: Wall Street Crash
sparks off Great Depression.
US and other economies
close to collapse.

1931

18 OCTOBER: Edison dies.
21 OCTOBER: USA turns off
electric lights as a mark of respect.

Glossary

Battery
An object that stores electricity.

Celluloid film
A substance on which images can be recorded.

Circuit
A system of transporting electricity.

Civil War
A war between different groups of people within one country.

Credit
A loan. If you buy something on credit, you take the goods and pay later.

Diaphragm
A thin skin that vibrates in response to sound.

Dynamo
A device for converting movement into electricity.

Electric current
The movement of electricity from one place to another.

Electrical pulses
Bursts of electrical current.

Electro-mechanician
A person who works on mechanical devices that use electricity.

Electromagnet
A magnet that works only when electrical current is passing through it.

Filament
A thin strip of material that lights up when electricty passes through it.

Generator
A device that turns heat into movement.

Industrial
To do with business, trade or manufacturing.

Low-grade
Low-grade metal ore is rock that does not contain much metal.

Manufactured
Made by people instead of occurring naturally.

Mechanical movement
The movement of a machine.

Morse code
A system of representing letters using dots and dashes.

Natural resources
Things such as coal or timber that occur naturally.

Patent
A patent is a legal document, which records the name of the inventor of a new idea.
It entitles the inventor to a share of any money made out of the idea.

Soliciting
To solicit something is to try to get it: a person soliciting your attention is trying to get you to pay them attention, for example.

Stock ticker
A telegraph-based device that transmitted news of the changes in the prices of stocks and shares.

Synchronize
To make things do the same thing at the same time; synchronized watches, for example, tell the same time.

Telegraph
A system of sending messages along a wire using Morse code.

Tramp telegrapher
Someone who moves from place to place working as a telegraph operator.

Transmitted
Sent.

Vacuum
A space in which there is nothing, not even air.

Vote counter
A device for counting votes.

Further Information

BOOKS FOR YOUNGER READERS

Bright Idea by Ann Moore
(MacDonald Young Books, 1997).
A story about Edison's daughter, Marion, who decides to find out exactly what her father does down in his basement laboratory, and witnesses one of his greatest achievements – the light bulb.

Thomas A. Edison by Anna Sproule (Exley, 1990).
Although it's now quite old, you can still find this book on library shelves. A highly readable account of Edison's life and major inventions.

Thomas Edison And Electricity by Steve Parker (Belitha Press, 1992), *Thomas Edison* by Nina Morgan (Wayland 1991) and *Thomas Edison* by Richard Tames (Franklin Watts 1990) are all straightforward accounts of Edison's life and inventions.

BOOKS FOR OLDER READERS

The best recent book on Edison is *Edison: A Life Of Invention* by Paul Israel (Wiley, 1998). Israel uses Edison's personal letters to give an insight into what he was thinking. The book is hard work because it's very long, but for anyone especially interested in a particular invention or episode it would be useful: there's a very good index.

WEBSITES

There are lots of Edison websites and most provide links to other sites. Here are a few to start with:

www.edisonian.com
Dedicated to early light bulbs and other inventions.

www.tinfoil.com
All about the invention of the phonograph.

www.edison.com/kids
A children's site dedicated to Thomas Edison.

www.edison-ford-estate.com
The official website of Edison's former home in Fort Myers, Florida.

Index

Page numbers in **bold** are pages where there is a photograph or an illustration.